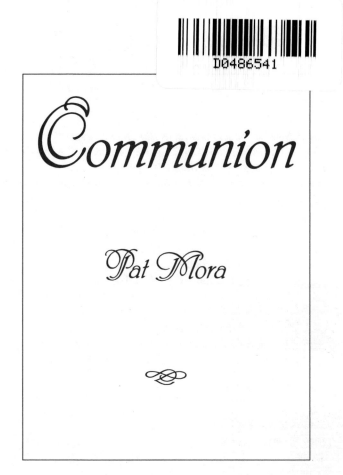

Communion

Pat Mora

Arte Publico Press
Houston
Texas
1991

Acknowledgements

This volume is made possible by a grant from the National Endowment for the Arts, a federal agency, and the Texas Commission on the Arts.

"Bosque del Apache" first appeared in *Blue Mesa Review*.
"Besham Qila, Pakistan" and "Gold" first appeared in *The Seattle Review*.
"Rituals" first appeared in *Cincinnati Poetry Review*.
"Mini-novela: *Rosa y sus espinas*" first appeared in *Prairie Schooner*.

Arte Público Press
University of Houston
452 Cullen Performance Hall
Houston, Texas 77204-2004

Cover Design by Mark Piñón
Original painting by Nivia González:
"Composición con Luna y Tierra," Copyright © 1988

Mora, Pat.
   Communion / Pat Mora.
     p.   cm.
   Poems.
   ISBN 1-55885-035-X
   1. Title
   PS3563.07306   1991
   811'.54—dc20   91-305
                                           CIP

For my parents

Estella and Raúl Mora.

¡Qué corazones!

Contents

Communion

I.
Old Bones

Gentle Communion

Even the long-dead are willing to move.
Without a word, she came with me from the desert.
Mornings she wanders through my rooms
making beds, folding socks.

Since she can't hear me anymore,
Mamande ignores the questions I never knew
to ask, about her younger days, her red
hair, the time she fell and broke her nose
in the snow. I will never know.

When I try to make her laugh,
to disprove her sad album face, she leaves
the room, resists me as she resisted
grinning for cameras, make-up, English.

While I write, she sits and prays,
feet apart, legs never crossed,
the blue housecoat buttoned high
as her hair dries white, girlish
around her head and shoulders.

She closes her eyes, bows her head,
and like a child presses her hands together,
her patient flesh steeple, the skin
worn, like the pages of her prayer book.

Sometimes I sit in her wide-armed
chair as I once sat in her lap.
Alone, we played a quiet I Spy.
She peeled grapes I still taste.

She removes the thin skin, places
the luminous coolness on my tongue.
I know not to bite or chew. I wait
for the thick melt,
our private green honey.

Senior Citizen Trio

They carry their words into the activity room,
scrubbed air, four walls bare of decoration,
no grace—but theirs. On sidewalk gray
January days, three students warm themselves
with coffee, survivors' smiles, and once-upon-
a-time Depression tales of empty pockets,
dinners of meat and potatoes, without the meat.

They read to one another, hands and words tremble
a bit, and then the catch in the throat, his tears
surprising them, and him. His apologies magnified
by hearing aids.

"I never thought I'd cry about it," he says.
"I was twelve then, so long ago, skinny kid
selling newspapers on a cold corner,
and Nini, my Italian friend, invited me
into his loud house. His family laughed at my
thin face, wedged me between thick shoulders
at the crowded table, gave me wine, a nickname,
spaghetti. At my Lutheran house, we never
drank, and we frowned at strangers."

He laughs, but his body cries again.
He apologizes, reads his last sentence,
"Thank God," but his body cries again,
"for Italians."

The two women know all about tears.
"Vell," says Helen who came from Hungary,
at forty, peeled grapes into fruit cocktail
while she learned English, "Vell," she says,
"You vere lucky."

Marty, one of eleven children who never saw
her mother's face, who brings the picture
of the daughter she buried last year, says,
"We won't live forever, ya know.
It's good to save the stories."

Señora X No More

Straight as a nun I sit.
My fingers foolish before paper and pen
hide in my palms. I hear the slow, accented echo
    How are yu? I ahm fine. How are yu?
of the other women who clutch notebooks
and blush at their stiff lips resisting
sounds that float gracefully as
bubbles from their children's mouths.
My teacher bends over me, gently squeezes
my shoulders, the squeeze I give my sons,
hands louder than words.
She slides her arms around me:
a warm shawl, lifts my left arm
onto the cold, lined paper.
"*Señora*, don't let it slip away," she says
and opens the ugly, soap-wrinkled fingers
of my right hand with a pen like I pry open
the lips of a stubborn grandchild.
My hand cramps around the thin hardness.
"Let it breathe," says this woman who knows
my hand and tongue knot, but she guides,
and I dig the tip of my pen into that white.
I carve my crooked name, and again at night
until my hand and arm are sore,
I carve my crooked name,
my name.

Stubborn Woman

You know her.
She keeps walking.

Even at eighty
when her knees ache
and she needs a winter coat in May,
she keeps walking.

Even when her ankles swell,
her bones frail fingernails,
her heart uphill
louder than car horns,
she keeps walking.

She buys thick heels, takes slow steps,
her pale eyes still gauging the safe route.
She pushes her grumbling body on.
She tells it:
we can browse stores whenever we want.
We can buy Listerine, mints, that new
cream that removes wrinkles, cologne
if it's on sale.

Divisadero Street, San Francisco

I watch a woman play with light,
at ease with the loud
orange of nasturtiums running
unchecked among the prim-
rose and the purple bursts of lillies of the Nile
in the cement heart of the city,
at ease with the sprawl of cats
and children wherever she kneels;
a woman who starts trees from seeds,
smells memories: the scent
of frilled rose geraniums becomes
the bubble-pop of apple jelly
she once scented with such frills. She sniffs
the pollen-heavy air for last year's bees.
Lost without dirt, she says,
so she greens this hidden square.

Light, ignored by the four straight backs
of buildings, gathers and shimmers
on the faces of daisies and poppies
open to the throat, light   dazzles
until we too shimmer.

Callas offer tall flutes of soothing cream.
I watch the woman, a tender
of possibilities, daily squeeze
one more stem into her plot.

Still Life

Still hearing dawn
alive with birds
stirring the morning breeze.

Still warming my fingers
round a cup, *café* I made
in the quiet
before the world fills the air.

Still opening these doors
heavier now
with my own, old hands,
weathered brown on brown.

Still holding soles and hammer
mending leather stubborn as my palms
                gently drumming
                gently drumming.

Still sweeping slowly as the sun
sets before I walk to the *plaza*
to watch the stars come out,
to watch the girls.

Spring again.

Two Women

They had opted for laughing,
the two women who nodded again and again
like ceramic figures that bob
at the touch, old friends
sharing wine and life's fears
laughing tears back.

The sun set and couples drifted in
the old two-by-two,
pale candles swaying on white lace.

      If one day we're widows, said one,

      if one day we're widows
            and alone

      can we share a home
      walk slowly arm-in-arm in the evening,

      maybe in the spring
      when the cholla shimmers
      dance together in the white of the moon?

for Tey Diana Rebolledo

Desert Pilgrimage

A few more steps, old feet.
Tonight I'll simmer dandelions
picked early this morning.
In pale tea I'll see
me with her, tasting wild grapes
at dawn, tasting dew
on tender leaves, another year.

I'll see us picking berries
to sprinkle in our soup,
all day harvesting desert herbs
her hands still guiding me,
at sunset grinding seeds
to thicken our stew.

I'll see us sitting
two boulders in the dark
listening   listening
watching stars tumble onto the sand
scattering white glowing
midnight blooms, a scent
I dream for months.

Tomorrow I'll store
creosote leaves to soothe
sore throats, and golden
pollen crystals, incense
I burn all year to hear her voice.

Don Jaime

In the pale tangle of light and leaf,
rocks and pebbles tumble,
ringing in the dawn like clay bells
as Don Jaime shuffles down the *monte*
glowing and dew-drenched as verbena
and salvia that curl around the lattice
of his fingers, wild cures sprouting roots
in the loam of his palms. The lame healer
and his grandson drag their basket brimming
with the rustle of branches and bark,
with *botón de oro*, flowers yellow as canaries,
the hot perfume an irresistible honey,
dizzying butterflies that doze
on the bodies and basket of this harvest
of faith, on these hands brimming
with ancient teas, pale green steam
which if inhaled with closed eyes
make us wonder
where we've been.

monte: large hill
botón de oro: creeping double-flowered crow-foot

Other Journeys

A white dwarf
soft hump, drooping ears,
loose, swaying chin, a dewlap,
thick, bull's body
pressed on stubby legs,

a white dwarf,
unnoticed in the red
and orange shouts of a Delhi bazaar,
Brahman dwelling oddly in my head
that doubts the memory,

seen at a glance
yet how such creatures lure us
into worlds gnarled and wild
as banyan trees, worlds of lizards
rising on hind legs, and butterflies,
heavy as eagles, rising

the white bull
nose moist, breath warm
still stares at me,
beckons

Arte popular

A hot breath among the pale crystal,
and polite watercolors of this tidy museum,
a breathing
in these new rooms,
and   faint drums, whistles, chants.

Judas figures puffed with sins rise
to the ceiling ready to explode into
pure white smoke,
dragons' eyes bulge, and green claws reach
to pull your hair
as masks sneer down
at skeletons dressed as bride and groom.

In Mexican villages
wrinkled hands lure and trap
dark spirits,
snakes
        slide into woven reeds
dogs
        growl softly in wood
frogs
        blow their wet song into clay flutes
jaguars
        pant in papier mache

a breathing   those spirits poised
to inhale deeply, fly out museum windows,
leap down steps three at a time, slither
on cool white marble into the night, into the full moon.

Foreign Spooks

Released full-blast into the autumn air
from trumpets, drums, flutes,
the sounds burst from my car like confetti
riding the first strong current.

The invisible imps from Peru, Spain,
Mexico grin as they spring from guitars,
harps, hand claps, and violins,

they stream across the flat fields of Ohio,
hide in the drafts of abandoned gray barns,
and the shutters of stern, white houses,

burrow into cold cow's ears and the crackle
of dry corn, in squirrel fur, pond ripple, tree gnarl,
owl hollow, until the wind sighs

and they open their wide, impudent
mouths, and together *con gusto*
startle sleeping farm wives,
sashaying raccoons, and even
the old harvest moon.

con gusto: with delight

Sweet Wine

The hurricane taught us a new breeding technique.
                                        Lepidopterist

Since no wings could outrace the wind,
blind as anger that pulled waves into
clouds, hurled sand through skin and skulls,
shredded trees like tissue paper,

the gold butterflies pressed
into mango and papaya rotting
in the grasses the fruitwine so sweet
the butterflies just sucked
and sucked deep in the soft flesh
deaf to the wind as it flung houses
and snarled away.

Warmly tipsy, those winged creatures
laughed without a sound
rolled over into a sleep thick as nectar,
and when the moon rose
they tumbled all
night, silent, amorous whirls.

The Taj Mahal

Like love it rises

between two mosques
thick roots concealed
        it floats
the Yamuna River braiding
behind it as day opens
and women wade into the gray,
rub water on their faces
bend again and again
into the Yamuna, their saris
heavy as they pound their wash,
float gold and purple
clothes on the glisten
watched by vultures meditating
on the banks, hawks circling
round the dome, circling gardens
where chipmunks and parrots
gather in the drizzle
that brushes this pearl
splashed with jade, vermilion, lapis
rising above the lovers' bones
        as all love rises
deceivingly simple,
the marble   rising

above legends of Mumtaz Mahal
'Light of the Palace'
dying in childbirth,
her husband's beard fading
marble-white within hours,
his sighs heavy as the scent

of mogra, flower intoxicating
as the moon.

Such love we all know
rising between us

some mornings shimmering
like a lotus
floating in this earth.

Bosque del Apache Wildlife Refuge

if the earth's old bones smile
I hear them
in the hush of this greenless forest
shining up to the gray clump of salt cedar
to black swords of mesquite
to the grace of grasses, yellow, rust

if the earth's old bones smile
I hear them shining
to strange chirps and chatters
to strange birds with necks that flow and flow
Canadian geese, sandhill cranes
stirring the air, stirring the air

if the earth's old bones smile
I hear them shining
in pools, in the mallard's green shimmer
in the startled   FLAP
filling the blue with a whirl white
silent, vast
then dip of black tip
snow geese, snow geese

if the earth's old bones smile
I hear them
shining in the white of the majestic crane
the great Whoop
white neck flowing, flowing
into desert grasses
white flowing
into the smile of old bones.

II.

Espinas

The Flood: A Huichol Myth

His feet were strangers,
unseen beneath the water rising up
his legs, his world now a brown
ocean deepening in the endless rain,
the sun fading like his memories
of leaves and faces, melting
in the streaming water, hers
the only other body still breathing,
her barks weakening,
her eyes glazing in the mist
when he finally pulled her and his unseen
feet into the lone boat, her fur-heavy body
sinking into the wood shell
that cupped them like a pair
of damp hands. The sky, a huge
gray gourd high above them, blackened,
the gray light vanishing,
the water streaming.

Day. Night. Gray. Black. Gray. Black
and then silence.

He scooped out the last of the cold
water and lay next to her, sank
into her wet fur, slid
into the only warmth in the world.
She gazed at him with her usual patience
and with her right paw
gently stroked his muddy face.

He woke when a pale sun rubbed his eyes,
and her hand—not her paw now, her hand
rubbed his lip. All day he studied her
almost hairless body. They listened to the sun
drying the watery world until the man and woman
could walk again on wet sand. They planted,
and one warm night she lay on the bed
of tender leaves he'd made for her, and she
again gave him what she could, their babies
carried safe in her since that first night,
now struggled into this empty world
whimpering, like puppies.

Year after year he sank into her
now familiar fur, into their private
dampness, and they whispered
with the leaves about the time
she stroked his cheek with her paw,
about the great rain.

Huichol: indigenous group in Mexico

Below the Surface

The man journeyed into the green hum
of heat, brushed damp earth from ancient
rock faces in the flap of parrots.

He shared hot mangoes with monkeys
and spoke to them night after night
under a loud moon of women in that other jungle
who ate him inside out, their teeth hidden behind
tender smiles. "Like yours," he'd say and laugh
at eyes gleaming down at him through the trees.

He planted his feet firmly on the familiar
green cush of fern and leaf at dawn,
his cry at the damp nail piercing
his shoe: private, unheard like his old love pains.

Trees spun and spun as he pulled the nail,
pounded his foot until it bled, knowing
we live alone and sometimes to save ourselves,
we have to rip our wounds open with our bare hands.

Veiled

If before the *mullah*'s morning call,
we tiptoe through the village
gather *burqas* that shroud
even the eyes,
        heavy, dark, like storm clouds

if we rush to the river
float the black and brown
garments on soft waves,
close our eyes, listen

will the water loosen
laughter trapped inside those threads,
will light songs rise
and swirl with the morning mist

or will sighs rise,
        heavy, dark like storm clouds?

mullah: Muslim leader of prayers
burqa: body-length veil

Besham Qila, Pakistan

Dusk: lights like fireflies
across the Indus
sliding, swirling gray
women
turquoise and gold figures
  wind their way
    down the patchwork slope
        scoop water cool as
        laughter into jars
        balanced lightly
    on their heads
   wind their way back
  into the dark
disappear again
into sod houses
safe like veils
and layers of soft
clothes wrapped to hide

the skin

nocturnal
each night swallowed
by the black mountain
     massive, hunched
     like the shoulders
     of a stubborn man.

Too Many Eyes

Once high in the Karakorams,
in a wooden stall perched
on the edge of a wild, churning river,
I modeled a white *shalwar kameez*
for you and twenty uninvited men
who stared, mouths open,
one almost toothless.

> Once on the eve of Eid,
> on a sizzling street
> I tasted sweet
> white candy and the stares
> of fifty uninvited men
> who watched my lips,
> hungrily, mouths open.

Horseflies, those eyes
nipped at my unveiled skin
day after day, wearied me
until I, a vain woman,
avoided mirrors and make-up,
pulled my hair back
with one quick twist,
hid in my wrinkled clothes.

Karakorams: mountain range in Pakistan
shalwar kameez: Pakistani shirt and trousers
Eid: Islamic religious observance

Khajuraho

"Rupee, rupee"
   words like light bells,
   ring behind us
      bangled wrists, small
      cupped hands,
"ruppee, rupee,
one, two, four,
nine, rupee, rupee,"

   ringing in the tiny village
   white sun slipping
   into the still lake

   nearby sculptured hands, breasts,
   hips, and tongues of Khajuraho,
   temples still hot

   like Hermavati, legend says,
   who tossed in the sheets
   one summer night walked barefoot
   to a pool, stroked
   gleaming ripples with her fingertips
   slipped out of her heavy clothes
      as Chandra, the Moon God watched,
   swam among the lotus,
   her skin whiter and whiter
   as Chandra slipped down
   into the water, into her

   whose son became King of Khajuraho.

   Now pilgrims and tourists stare
   at these temples, these figures

that touch and taste openly,
fingers and mouths almost moving
on the hot walls,
a spell about the temple garden
and village as if the mix
of jasmine and flesh drugs us so,

the young voices pure as bells,

"rupee, rupee,"
become an alien sound.

Frenzy

safe they looked
roosting in a tree   the chickens
sinking into their feathers
sinking into the velvet night

the DRUM
the singing, mouths opening and opening
Cuban dancers   swaying their hips
into one another, sliding up and down
bodies   loose
yelling from the stage into our dark

the DRUM, the drum louder,
the dancer   prowling
his eyes searching
inside our clothes
and no escape
vulnerable as chickens

the DRUM, the drum quickening his breaths
the chicken
stretched tight as my neck
a woman's teeth sinking, sinking into feathers

                                       blood

poured from the neck into
a cheap cup   and rum
rumblood
poured down our throats

DRINK
said with unparted lips
he   moving heavily around us
hitting our backs   hard
hitting our pale fear
yanking us
onto the stage for   a cleansing, *una limpieza*

the DRUM,
inside my neck
louder, louder
eggs swept over our bodies
to lure out evil
our bodies sinking
into the smell of pineapple, mangoes,
drums, heat
heat, heat
yellow, ripe

The Mystery

In Cuba women smile all day
while they cook rice and beans in hot, tiny kitchens.
They smile while they rock on the long bus ride
to work, while they iron wrinkled tobacco leaf
after leaf with their hands hour after hour
listening to loud speakers throbbing with *revolución*.
They smile while they shop in empty
stores that sell only brown skirts, only brown
shoes and when they touch my new purse
shy as children. They smile when they tell of gifts:
scented soaps, silk slips smooth on their skin once
from California, a word they stretch like gum
on the tongue. They smile when their children march
by in uniform, all in step, all smiling.

On Fire

He holds girls' voices
the way we hold crystal
when we spin its prisms in the sun.

Aware they can't bear
to more than glance at his patched
skin, he holds what he can, their voices

allows himself to ask the question
only three times a day, "Got the time?"
asks the pretty ones whose laughs shine

until they are close enough
to see his dry, white skin, stretched
like a thin quilt pieced from his own scraps

onto his bones by doctors who know
about fire, whose hands know him.
He longs to touch the laughing girls,

their smooth, polished, glowing surfaces,
to rub his skin on all that softness,
the moving curves.

He stands there silent in the sun
holds each voice, strokes its clear
rising, light whispers between his sad thighs.

Perfume

How do we scrub away this blood,
how do we scrub away this hot smell
before the children run up the path
chasing one another—one, two
three, four voices, "*Mamá*
                        Mamá"
ready to hug her,
stomach sliced open
one, two, three, four times.

Maybe her perfume this morning
was too strong for the man
who once beer-laughed night after night,
lately thinner, tired, until she went
to work to buy groceries, medicines.

"Slut," he'd yell, "you only want
to laugh with other men."
"Whore," he'd mutter staring
at the ceiling above their bed,
day after day hearing her laugh
slip through the cracks onto his skin—
though she worked miles away.

Maybe her perfume this morning
was too strong, and he locked the doors,
chased her with that knife
        slash / slash
        slash / slash
never hearing her scream
even at the end when she held her
stomach with both hands trying to hold

her life in as he stabbed himself,
        though not well enough,
yelled, "*La maté*: I've killed Gloria."

Gloria.
Lost inside her useless body.

What do we do with her four?
Fall and spring they'll look for her
at the *mercado*, in crowded stores,
they'll see her back and then
she'll vanish again and again.

They'll whisper to her at night,
dream she's in the other room
worried, looking for them.
They'll wake shaking in the dark,
crying, "*Mamá! Mamá!*"

mercado: market

Emergency Room

he clothed me in bruises
socked and slapped   socked and slapped

                                earlier i'd powdered
my arms   legs   slipped on
my soft   green dress
                                only nice dress
            sweet smell
hot bus   men   bumping into me
hot line at the agency
me saying   *sí   sí*
over and over in my head
skin on fire
forms   blanks   my ugly
writing telling them
            i want to work
our apartment shrinking
in on me   on me   him

saw the green dress on the bed
asked why   i

so i dont cover my breasts
with my hands or a white sheet
no
you can look and touch
i m blue neck to knee
he clothed me in bruises

Old Anger

I didn't believe he loved that woman,
didn't believe he stroked her
cheek softly when she dreamed, wrapped himself
around her in the cold.

Ella. She lured him away from me
and the children years ago, into her
perfume, powder, soft, inviting skin
that held him even at the end
when she coughed herself away night after night.

But when she died, he shuffled head down
through the *rancho* with the coffin,
weaving like a dry leaf in the wind,
stood alone by her grave, wiped a tear away.
They saw. All eyes saw my *hombre macho*
wipe a tear away.

My daughters lured him back into our house.
They plead, "Speak to him. It's Christmas. For us."
Ten years he has shuffled through these rooms,
but I live alone, inside myself.

My old anger warms my bones.

ella: she
rancho: small village
hombre: man

Abuelita's Ache

Celia watches him with the green eyes
of a woman in love, watches him laugh
and strut free through the market
a loose rooster sqawking
while her love grows tendrils
tangling inside her.

Blind old woman am I who didn't see
how carefully she braids her hair
now hoping to braid him
tight to her. And her morning face
pale as old sheets? And her loose clothes?
Blind old woman am I. *Ay. Ay. Ay.*

Village snakes will hiss-hiss
"Celia's secret's blossoming, blossoming."
Each day I want to pile the vegetables we sell
higher and higher, to hide my sweet, foolish girl
in the green dark, to sing to her
like I did when I rocked her to sleep in my arms,
　　　rru-rru-que-rru-rru
lullabies she will need soon enough.

abuelita: grandmother

Rituals

Our children came for our hands,
for the last blessing, came to memorize our faces,
our wrinkled bark. One by one they returned
to the *rancho* on that grumbling bus. I felt
the faces I no longer see, traced eyebrows, nose,
lips, gently pressed their eyelids, felt their life
flicker on my fingertips.

The house was noisy again, the arguing, loud pigeons
flapping. My husband shouted orders, missing the sound
of his own voice. He showed our sons the bags of cement
to seal us on all sides so we will lie clean
in that hole. He sent the youngest to Santa Maria
for the coffins, said to store corn and beans in them
until we die. A safe, dry place. He gave our sons
his hoe and pick, but said, *"Oigan, muchachos.*
I know my young one drinks too much beer.
Touch him and no locks will keep me out."

My startled birds left the thorny nest again.
My husband is all bones now, even cotton pants
wear him out. All day we linger at our door.
My days are nights. I've learned to feel my way.

rancho: small village
oigan, muchachos: listen, boys

Sueños: Dreams

She dreams her hands are feathered.
On the dirt floor, curled between
Coke crates, cardboard boxes,
and her clay menagerie, under the green
bananas hanging on a line away from
dogs, rats, and brothers,
as clouds seep into the adobe bricks,
stroke her ankles caked with mud,
her patched clothes, tangled hair,
she dreams the clay birds and butterflies
still wet in her hands, stir, flutter, lift
their wings like petals opening
on a hot afternoon, and she too
rises into the sun
light as a dandelion plume,
in silent laughter tumbles, glides.

Fences

Mouths full of laughter,
the *turistas* come to the tall hotel
with suitcases full of dollars.

Every morning my brother makes
the cool beach sand new for them.
With a wooden board he smooths
away all footprints.

I peek through the cactus fence
and watch the women rub oil
sweeter than honey into their arms and legs
while their children jump waves
or sip drinks from long straws,
coconut white, mango yellow.

Once my little sister
ran barefoot across the hot sand
for a taste.

My mother roared like the ocean,
"No. No. It's their beach.
It's their beach."

The Other Woman

There's a woman who searches
your trash for ribbons and eggs,
hovers unseen around your knees,
shines your shoes and cabinets
until you can see your face
everywhere, your world, a mirror.
She holds your baby in one arm
while you play the piano,
your fingers cool, smooth ivory,
and when you leave, she dances
in your dress berry-red,
a ring on every finger.
She sips a bit of wine.

Back home this woman cooks
enough for ten, rubs her mother's feet
with hot ointment, sleeps under
children who burrow, steamy animals
in the dark. This woman dances
only with her brothers.

Mini-novela: *Rosa y sus espinas*

Empty as I feel, this house,
only four children left, and horseflies,
always the whine of horseflies.

Afternoons I suck candies,
and watch *novelas*, watch
goldenwomen startling as a full moon.

A *novela* of my life would be called
Rosa y sus espinas or maybe The Whine.

Episode I: The Fires

Young, he and I scurry barefoot, heads down,
into the night green with ripe corn,
hiding in cornsilk, in the rustle
of his father's fields. Cautious
as rats, we roast corn under cold
stars, grind our teeth into
cobs we gnaw without tasting,
frantic after hours of water, only water.

All day at the big house, dog tongues
lap rice and meat, while in our *jacal*
we count each bean and kernel she sends,
stingy as this dry dirt, his mother,
waiting for him to leave my *jacal*, and me.

Nights our fingers bury ashes, the black
stain year after year, hiding
our fires, the little ones
also scurrying barefoot, one two, three,
four, five, six, seven, eight, nine, ten,

eleven heads down, hiding in the cornsilk
of their grandfather's fields after a day
of water, water, water, their whine,
the horseflies' whine.

Episode II: The Other Woman

They scuffle in a cave near the *rancho*,
their moans soft, warm breezes.
My husband kisses her so hard her split, swollen
lips hide in her rosary for days. She bewitches

tequila, murmurs over
candles and bottle, murmurs over him,
his eyes and mouth ready for her as she
pours fire.

When he returns home he is cobweb
white. His skin splits and our eleven watch
a swarm of creatures, small pollen
feed silently on his wounds, his hands too weak
to brush fragile wings from his eyes.

Twelve months I drag him to doctors,
to *curanderos* who only stare at my man,
my shrinking autumn leaf.

I drag him from *rancho* to *rancho*,
each month he's lighter, drying.
Alone I bury his body, small like my babies.
I bury him to the whine of horseflies.

Episode III: The Return

I drag my heavy bones back to the dark house
where my children stayed those long months.

Nose against the window I watch them
crawl into my mother's kitchen, cautious
as rats, they grind their teeth into soft
corn soaking on the table until

my mother's eyes fill the room with
green lightning. She slaps their mouths
like she slapped me once for stroking
my father's beard, soft as cornsilk.

My scream startles me. They wrap around
me. "*Mamá, Mamá*, where have you been?"
Their bones push into me, no womb big
enough, soft mouths say, "One dark, cold room,
no pillows, only one dry *tortilla* a day,
and water, water, water." I hear

horseflies breeding in my ears. I throw
what my hands find, soft tomatoes smack
into my mother's face. Seeds and pulp stick
to her silent lips.

My children scurry with me, barefoot,
heads down, into the night, into our old
jacal. I dream waves, waves of milk.

Episode IV: The Second Man

Cautious as rats, my children watch me
hide in the curtain like they hide in
mesquite, my game more dangerous.

My fingers stroke my face when I study
the man's beard each night, the new man
who knocks on my neighbor's door.

Under faded dresses, I find my old,
cracked mirror, re-learn my face, wish I
were slim as a new moon. One night
my eyes pull him in.
My children crouch, their eyes dart
at him, bite-bite,
the eyes of his children
and mother-in-law bite me.
But like that other man I buried,
small like my babies, he moves in,
no weddings, just men hiding their fires.

When he sleeps, I stroke his beard.
But the children bite-bite until
one day he slips away like a shadow.
Now I stroke my face to sleep.

Episode V: The Survival

In the early light the horseflies hover
and whine above the nest of arms and legs,
above the mouths moaning softly.

I slip out, envying birds,
their wings lively in the breeze
bear red berries to waiting mouths,
warm cups. I balance water heavy on my head.

Winters I pierce fat blisters
on our cold, cramped feet.
Summers I climb the hills,
gather what I can,

peel *tunas*, feed the seed pulp
that stains open mouths red

as the lipstick Lupe, my first,
smears on her lips, not yet sixteen.
She sways away to the bus
for the border, her feet cramped in
someone's scuffed high heels.

Episode VI: The Present

Each night I kneel and sway
with the candle and horseflies.
I pray the moon will turn her head
when Lupe scurries
barefoot, head down across the Rio Bravo.

Year by year my children wave
at me as the bus sways away. One by one
they scurry heads down across the *río*.
They send letters others read to me,
money, and pictures of pale babies. I

hear my last four whisper
about the day they'll leave, go across
the *río* to cities that never sleep.
I suck candies and watch *novelas*.
I raise the volume until
I can't hear the whine.

novela: soap opera
Rosa y sus espinas: Rose and her thorns
jacal: shack
tunas: fruit of the prickly pear cactus
curandero: folk healer

Picturesque: San Cristóbal de las Casas

No one told me about the bare feet.

The Indians, yes
the turquoise and pink shawls, yes
the men running lightly on thin sidewalks
hats streaming with ribbons, yes
the chatter of women sunning outside the church
weaving bracelets with quick fingers, yes

but no one told me about the bare feet.

The smiles, yes
the babies slung on women's backs,
the bundles of huge white lilies
carried to market: fresh headdresses,
the young girls like morning birds gathering
for a feeding, pressing dolls into my hands, yes

but no one told me about the bare feet.

The weavers, yes
the hands that read threads,
the golden strings pulled from bushes
in fresh handfuls to steal a yellow dye,
the houses in the clouds, in the high hills,
shuttles to-and-fro, to-and
-fro on tight looms, yes

but no one told me about the bare feet.
No one told me about the weaver's chair, a rock.
No one told me about the wood bundles bending
women's backs. No one told me about the children

who know to open their smiles
as they open their dry palms.

Dominican Gold

They wade into the river
each morning, sink bare feet
in the sand, lift thick sticks with two hands
and begin their sad, watery music.
They pound, pock the river's edge
with shallow holes into which they dip
wooden bowls, read the dregs like fortune
tellers reading tea leaves. The child glistens
nude in the river all day, scoops water
as his sister pounds to an internal rhythm
until she can't hear
voices or wind, just *slosh, slosh*
persistent as time, as her hunger pounding
inside her. The grandmother's damp clothes
cling to legs thinner than the sticks she plunges.
Her fingers, hungry snakes, slide
through the trapped water poised for a glint.

Each morning the family wades into the river
flowing with promise, away from dry
soil that yields only rocks they suck
instead of rice or *yuca* until that awaited day
when their hands, dark and knobby as wet twigs,
fill with a loud light.

yuca: cassava

Witness

She gathers quiet around her
like a shawl carried in a worn bag
from place to place, her fingers
checking often that it's by her side.

Throughout the day, she pauses
for a spell, gathers the familiar
scent and texture around
her shoulders and elbows.

Within its folds, she hears
a wail, a child's mouth bursts
open like his skin exploding in pain.

Within its folds, she hears
the earth sigh
at ancient trees uprooted,
at blooms shriveled in smoke.

Carefully she records the limbs,
still now in the heat, and then
she rises, gathers the stormy power
of forgotten spirits to her while we hush,
and as she speaks we feel our tongues,
heavy, hiding, unwilling to utter
the truths we know.

for Denise Levertov

Peruvian Child

Still in the middle of my path is the child
with no smile who stared at us. Her eyes
even then the eyes of women who sell chickens
and onions at outdoor markets. The women
who stare at us as if we are guards.

She whispered to the doll with no face,
smoothed the red and blue scraps
of cloth on the path, ironed them with her hand,
wrapped and re-wrapped the doll, hair
mud-tangled as the child's, and the dog's,
and the llama's that followed the child's
small bare feet after she bundled the doll
in the striped *manta* on her back.

The matted group stood by the edge of the spring
watching us drink clear, holy water of the Inca,
a fountain of youth, our guide said.
We wanted, as usual, to hold a picture
of the child in a white border, not to hold her
mud-crusted hands or feet or face,
not to hold her, the child in our arms.

manta: mantle

Tigua Elder

How do I tell my children:
there is worse than pain.

I bury pills.
Let my stomach burn.
I bury them in the sand by the window,
under the limp cactus.
Maybe it slipped into a long sleep instead of me.
I speak to my grandchildren in our language,
but they hear only television, radio
in every room, all day, all night.
They do not understand.

How do I tell my children:
forgetting is worse than pain, forgetting
stories old as the moon; owl, coyote,
snake weaving through the night like smoke,
forgetting the word for the Spirit,
waida, waida, the sound I hear in shells
and damp caves, forgetting the wind,
the necessary bending to her spring tantrums.

Afternoons I limp like a wounded horse
to the shade of the willow and wait for sunset,
for wind's breath, familiar, cool.
She eases this fire.

There is worse than pain.
There is forgetting
those are my eyes in the mirror.
There is forgetting my own true name.

Tigua: a Native American Southwestern group

The System

Mamá, night is never pure
black here. When the sun sets,
lights search the corners like ants
search the dry exercise yard. Eyes
here are jagged tin. They slice skin,
and what seeps out stinks worse
than the gray smell of boiled meat.

I step aside to let ants pass now.
I watch them, their nervous jerks,
their search for a dark corner
and one sweet orange. I watch their fragile
legs, their lines, silent, staring at
cement, thousands we never hear.

The Eye of Texas

is white
as sun-bleached bone,
its one eye, a star
between two long horns,
was once two new eyes
that stared at one another until
the young bull could see only itself
reflected in those huge, soft mirrors
that grew together, hardened, a scar white

as its hoofs that trample deserts,
valleys, fields, shores, country roads,
the bull pausing to raise its
thick neck, its one white eye to the unseen
sky and bellow louder than the combined cries
of *coyotes*, wolves, mountain lions,
bellowing a dark, bitter smoke
then charging on, crushing cotton, onions,
hierbabuena, trampling toys and children
in narrow dirt streets of the Rio Grande Valley,
deaf to the cries of old Mexican voices,

the bull seeking the smell of white
skin and chlorine, resting its loud body
by the acres of tinted, treated pools
owned by men who wrap their feet in snakes,
their legs in blue jeans, lull
the old, blind bull with their tales
tall as their hats that shade tongues
twanging like snapping guitar strings.

The one-eyed longhorn dreams of stomping
its hoofs hard on its land until
the only smell is white-
tongued, twanging children.

Order

If each family member gets one story,
his would be the day he swept the hawthorne
bush out back, a perfectly natural act
for a man who wore brooms out in a month,
who never opened windows, who scrubbed
all surfaces smooth.

We watched and waved at the window
that May morning, but his mouth was a stiff thorn
in the soft, surprising snow. With hard strokes
he swept door mats and patio as he did other days
to remove the irrepressible desert that drifted in
uninvited, casual as sin.

That morning he swept the white
bushes with his broom, an image I remembered
years later in India when I saw a man mowing
tender grasses growing out of a lake.

Daydreams: Traveler, Wife

1

Dozing in the warm perfume
                              jasmine, orange
you see me
gliding toward you
skimming countries and oceans

                                        with the tips
                                        of my bare toes
pulled by your silent call.

2

Remember the snake rhyme, snake rhyme
            red and yellow
            kill a fellow?
            I plot,
            black and yellow
                  scare a fellow.
My faraway dreamer
nearly napping
            I plot
                  to startle you
            burst
            black and yellow
                  on your knee
my feathers a gleaming ebony
eye
    a hard, bitter lemon
beak
    a hooked thorn.

You'd flinch
                at my claw-hold
                at my stare-glare
till you felt the chill
                        whispered: wife?

My beak would open slowly,
                        hiss, hiss.

New York: 2 a.m.

Your sleep and sirens,
night emergencies
persistent as this city's
horns and motor throbs,
as the cold feet padding
above us on patient carpets,
layers and layers of city
sleepers and wanderers
ignored by the pale, glowing
faces of clocks
that ignore me
coiled in a hotel chair,
silently repeating
complaints predictable as
penmanship exercises,
circling each of your familiar
sins in the catechism I write,
gliding around them
as I once rounded letters
savoring the familiar
without pause, gliding
onto the next, a litany
that always lulls you into
a dangerous sleep,
a moonless swamp.

Leaves breathe slowly near your face,
insistent roots coil up your legs,
two eyes pierce
you awake.

Probing

If we were a wound,
I'd slit us open with my sharpest knife,
or bite into us if necessary;
peer with a magnifying glass. I'd pour
warm water and then peroxide,
comforted by its froth. I'd probe
with a fine point, digging deeper
and deeper until the flesh began to bleed,
and then the peroxide again, the endless
digging, the tired cells unable to heal
under my fierce hands.

If we were a wound,
you'd quickly bandage us to avoid
the bloody mess. You'd look away and say,
"Remember Pakistan, the moonscape, the hard
mountains bare of grass or tree, the snow
in June, the night without light, the silent,
bearded men who shepherd goats, the forgotten
women hidden in layers of dark cloth who talk
endlessly to themselves, the waterfalls, and oh
the baths, canals, reservoirs I dig and probe,
the necessary water cooling and cleansing thousands."

III.
A Voice

The Conference Male

Why aren't they hoarse
these men who talk talktalktalk
tongues taptaptapping before
the first cup of coffee,
tongues polished and hard
like flamenco shoes demanding we hush.

Even at night
when no one else is in the room
does the talktalktalk tick on,
each tongue dancing proudly
for the bathroom mirror,
the viewer quick to clap clapclapclap?

A Voice

Even the lights on the stage unrelenting
as the desert sun couldn't hide the other
students, their eyes also unrelenting,
students who spoke English every night

as they ate their meat, potatoes, gravy.
Not you. In your house that smelled like
rose powder, you spoke Spanish formal
as your father, the judge without a courtroom

in the country he floated to in the dark
on a flatbed truck. He walked slow
as a hot river down the narrow hall
of your house. You never dared to race past him,

to say, "Please move," in the language
you learned effortlessly, as you learned to run,
the language forbidden at home, though your mother
said you learned it to fight with the neighbors.

You liked winning with words. You liked
writing speeches about patriotism and democracy.
You liked all the faces looking at you, all those eyes.
"How did I do it?" you ask me now. "How did I do it

when my parents didn't understand?"
The family story says your voice is the voice
of an aunt in Mexico, spunky as a peacock.
Family stories sing of what lives in the blood.

You told me only once about the time you went
to the state capitol, your family proud as if
you'd been named governor. But when you looked
around, the only Mexican in the auditorium,

you wanted to hide from those strange faces.
Their eyes were pinpricks, and you faked
hoarseness. You, who are never at a loss
for words, felt your breath stick in your throat

like an ice-cube. "I can't," you whispered.
"I can't." Yet you did. Not that day but years later.
You taught the four of us to speak up.
This is America, Mom. The undo-able is done

in the next generation. Your breath moves
through the family like the wind
moves through the trees.

Nuns

I couldn't resist the great folds of hushed
black into which they tucked all fleshy appendages

and floated, the white collars stiff as polished
ribs, the scrubbed faces, the rhythmic click,

click, click of beads familiar as the cricket.
At home I lined dining room chairs into perfect

rows like pews, hid my hair in a black *mantilla*,
swallowed white spongy bread I'd press flat

and round between my fingers. I waited
for the day I'd join their order so unlike

my irregular family that spoke Spanish
and ignored clocks. I picked a new name

for the me who would live in those black,
soap-smelling folds, those safe, uniform collars.

mantilla: shawl

The Young Sor Juana

I

I'm three and cannot play away my days
to suit my sweet *mamá*. Sleep well, my dolls,
for I must run to school behind my sister's frowns.
She knows my secret wish to stretch. If only
I were taller. If only I could tell *Mamá* why
I must go, my words irresistible as roses.

My sister hears my tiptoes, knows her shadow
has my face. I tiptoe on, for I must learn
to unknit words and letters, to knit them new
with my own hand. Like playful morning birds
the big girls giggle, at me, the little tagalong.
I hear the grumble of my sister's frown.

I stretch to peek inside, to see
the teacher's face. How it must glow with
knowledge. Like the sun. A woman so wise
has never tasted cheese. She sees my eyes
and finally seats me near. My stubborn legs
and toes refuse to reach the floor.

At noon I chew my bread. Others eat soft
cheese. I've heard it dulls the wits. I shut
my lips to it. I must confess, when tired,
I slowly smell the milky moons, like *Mamá*
savors the aroma of warm roses. I linger,
imagine my teeth sinking into the warm softness.

II

I'm seven and beg to leave my sweet *mamá*,
to hide myself inside boys' pants and shirt,
to tuck my long, dark hair inside a cap
so I can stride into large cities, into their
classrooms, into ideas crackling
and breathing lightning.

Instead of striding I must hide from frowns,
from dark clouds in the eyes of my *mamá*.
I hide in my grandfather's books, sink
into the yellowed pages, richer than cheese.
Finally *Mamá* releases me to her sister.
I journey to the city. If only I were taller.

III

I'm sixteen and spinning in the glare of Latin
grammar. I cannot look away. Beware,
slow wits, I keep my scissors close,
their cold, hard lips ready to sink into
this dark, soft hair, punish my empty head,
unless it learns on time.

I'll set the pace and if I fail, I'll hack and
slash again until I learn. I'll pull and cut,
this foolish lushness. Again I'll feel my hair
rain softly on my clothes, gather
in a gleaming puddle at my feet.
My hands are strong, and from within I rule.

sor: member of religious community, sister
Sor Juana Inés de la Cruz: seventeenth century author,
    Mexico's most acclaimed woman poet

Mothers and Daughters

The arm-in-arm-mother-daughter-stroll
in villages and shopping malls
evenings and weekends
the w a l k - t a l k slow,
arm-in-arm
         around the world.

Sometimes they feed one another
memories sweet as hot bread
and lemon tea. Sometimes it's mother-stories
the young one can't remember:

"When you were new, I'd nest you
in one arm, while I cooked,
whisper, what am I to do with you?"

Sometimes it's tug
-of-war that started in the womb
the fight for space
the sharp jab deep inside
as the weight shifts,
arm-in-arm
         around the world

always the bodytalk thick,
always the recipes
hints for feeding
more with less.

Teenagers

One day they disappear
into their rooms.
Doors and lips shut,
and we become strangers
in our own home.

I pace the hall, hear whispers,
a code I knew but can't remember,
mouthed by mouths I taught to speak.

Years later the door opens.
I see faces I once held,
open as sunflowers in my hands. I see
familiar skin now stretched on long bodies
that move past me
glowing almost like pearls.

Cissy in a Bonnet

You wore your brain backwards,
the bonnet you called your brain
at four years old, pulled the yellow
ties to frame your face, the floppy useless brim
bobbing behind your head as you ran free.

At fourteen you frown and turn
away from the pictures, and us.
"You let me look like that?" you ask
again marveling at the ineptitude of parents.

The bonnet travels with me
wherever I move, a nondisposable artifact
for your eventual backwards journey below
your bones, for the day you study the family
album and finger the bonnet alone, maybe
pull it on, the ties dangling foolishly
around your careful face, a yellow clue
as you search next in the mirror
for the girl who laughed with her clothes.

Maybe part of the journey is always backwards,
the careful brushing away of the layers,
personal archaeology, uncovering forgotten,
broken pieces, sifting even in our dreams
until we fit the jagged edges into round wholes
we cherish privately; and occasionally we
break the code, with our fingers read our early
symbols, reunite with the rare spirits we house.

The Old Crone

Black bandana hid her hair,
long I'm sure, and gray. She was slightly bent,
tongue sharper than her eyes—
and they missed nothing.

My scold muttered her days away
inside me, asked, "Why don't you bake fresh bread,
bury egg shells and orange rind for compost,
stir great pots of soup seasoned green
with herbs from your garden, wash windows
until they vanish, cure your children's coughs
with cups of hot *hierbabuena* at night
lock all doors and windows,
like a great hen, fluff your layers and doze
inside, inside?"

Once her voice was loud:
        "Away and alone, away and alone,"
she muttered as I boarded plane
after plane, rocked on foreign subways by myself.
        "Unwanted, unwanted,"
she chanted the first time I said,
"Table for one," words bitter
as a spoiled olive splitting in my mouth.

Oh, she was stubborn, nagged
me day and night, but she grew weary,
began dozing more and more
which let me study her at rest,
see how small she was. Now
she sleeps for months at a time.

hierbabuena: mint tea

Seminar

Words fell like snow
numbed my feet slowly
clung to the hem
of my cotton skirt
soaked into my blouse
and gathered on my shoulder
until I could barely raise
my hand, heavy like my
eyes, so I slipped
away alone down the green
hill to the lake
         the melt
sweet as red wings lifting
from the brambles, as the flight.

Silence Like Cool Sand

First lie in it.
Close your eyes.
Let it move through you.
Rock your shoulders back and forth.
Dig your heels in.
Slow your breath.

Curl forward and wash
your hands with it.
Pour it slowly on your legs.
Rub your heels deeper
into the damp.
Bury your toes.
Roll back, eyes shut.
Disappear into it.
Listen to the scratchings, then listen,
listen to the roar.

Tree-wisdom

Its steady claws dig
deep. Center it.
Ten of us can't budge
its weathered,
stubborn trunk.

Yet its limbs are moved by every brush of flesh,
feather, fur. Even a baby's breath starts a shiver
shimmering into the drowsy steam.
Those limbs, like moon-drunk flamenco gypsies, stretch
their gold, green, and garnet bangles into wind
wails, whirl wild when thunder claps.

Still, a tree moves, trembles
at the invisible. Without lungs or lips,
whispers and howls.

In wise rhythm, a tree retreats,
strips to feed itself.

But when the sap springs, a tree's bones burn
green. How it swells, then, a mass of praise.
A tree surprises itself, year after year,
climbs its rings,
climbs itself.

My Word-house

The walls grow out of the desert
naturally, like *agave, nopal,* yucca.
Vines, winds, and strangers enter large, bare
rooms with ease, no private entrances, no secret locks,
just rough *álamo* slabs framing windows and doors.

In the center courtyard water murmurs
as canaries and parrots teach desert sparrows
to swim, to rainbow the fountain's ripples
with feathers, to sink for long naps into cool
mud, into the lap of water. Koi, gold and orange,
gleam from high leaves, glide with their fins from tree
to tree building perfumed nests of veined lavender petals.

Men and women pull threads from
their mouths, soak the strong fibers in berries,
roots, shells, then weave them as the wind loosens
songs. In the kitchen family bread is always rising.

Since the desert moon can't resist the warm aroma
of *flamboyán,* each night she slides to mirrored
pillows near the marimba and sitar, rises on bare
feet, dances with other white-haired women,
all their long, loose hair glimmering
as they teach smooth, small soles
the deep pulse hot in the sand.

Sleepy, the young wash feet that taught
the dance, rub knots and gnarls they'll own.
Bodies and butterflies rest in the slow breaths
of water. *La luna* hums with the earth's dark
rhythms, hums lullabies of yellowed lace.

nopal: prickly pear
álamo: cottonwood
flamboyán: flowering tree, royal poinciana
la luna: the moon

Tejedora maya

You too know the persistent buzz
of white space, stubborn as a fly,
the itch. My white is paper,
yours is cotton cloth you smooth
with rough palms in the shade of the old tree,
feel designs alive,
a braile we can't see,
butterflies, scorpions, snakes
darting and tumbling in your dreams
brushing the backs of your eyes
slither to your fingertips, dart
into red and black threads
      your hands, your mother's hands
      your grandmother's hands
unleash frogs and flowers
older than your bones.

tejedora: weaver

Dream Babies

Night after night I hold them
in my dreams and say the words.
They fit on my hip, warm
as yeast dough, a sturdy weight
steadying me as faces concrete as
clouds turn around us. I breathe them in,
the baby skin, the lips curling hungrily
around the word-shapes, mouthing
  ball, balloon, spoon, moon
our breaths loosening, a duet.

One night the baby was black.
I asked permission to adopt her,
waited for my children's votes.
Night or day I count them. The first
fresh flesh to fill my arms fit
like the welcome weight
of water in a thirsty cup.

We count, tonight's baby and I
  one, two, three
cheek to cheek, our breaths blow warm,
mix sweet as lavender and mint,
my voice/her voice/our voice
  brown, black, or white
mysterious as yeast, rises.

Strong Women

Some women hold me when I need to dream,
rock, rocked my first red anger through the night.
Strong women teach me courage to esteem,

to stand alone, like cactus, persevere
when cold frowns bite my bones and doubts incite.
Some women hold me when I need to dream.

They walk beside me on dark paths I fear,
guide with gold lanterns: stories they recite.
Strong women teach me courage to esteem.

They watch me stumble on new trails I clear.
In hope, feed me their faith, a warm delight.
Some women hold me when I need to dream.

In their safe arms, my visions reappear:
skyfire voices soar, blaze, night ignite.
Strong, women teach me courage to esteem.

They sing brave women, sisters, we revere
whose words seed bursts of light that us unite.
Some women hold me when I need to dream.
Strong women, teach me courage to esteem.

Dar a luz

I am gathering myself
like I gather myself after sex
reaching to touch a leg, arm, hand
and fingers to help me grasp
the water I sip to bless me whole again.

I am gathering my
fear of a room bare of any voice but mine,
stories wise as old bells tolling in my blood,
swelling silence—hard, bitter, green,
that ripens, glows.

I am gathering myself
to triumph, not like a warrior collects
boots, helmet, bayonet, gun, grenades.
No. I am gathering light, not from the moon
or sun. No, I am gathering from within,
a light safe to follow.

dar a luz: to give birth